Carla's A

Book 1 of the Travelling Trunk Series

Carla's Adventure in Guatemala

Missy Tarantino

Illustrations by Ian Smiley

Copyright © 2019 by Melissa Tarantino
All rights reserved. This book or any portion thereof may not be reproduced or used in any manner whatsoever
without the express written permission of the author except for the use of brief quotations in a book review.

Contact the author at:

https://missytarantino.com/

or

Honeybee Publishing; LLC
PO Box 12
Ault, CO 80610

Printed in the United States of America

First Printing, 2019

This book is dedicated to my nephew, Denis.

You were the inspiration for this story. I love you!

Acknowledgements: I would like to thank my students, especially Vianca, Leticia, Ever, and Gaspar, who were all born in Guatemala, for reading my manuscript and helping to make it great. I am so grateful that I get to work with you each and every day.

Table of Contents

Chapter 1 .... Boredom

Chapter 2 .... The Traveling Trunk

Chapter 3 .... Antigua

Chapter 4 .... The Worry Doll

Chapter 5 .... Fiesta!

Chapter 6 .... Kite Festival

Chapter 7 .... The Necklace

Chapter 8 .... Going Back Home

Chapter 9 .... The Sticker

Hello Readers!

I hope you enjoy this first story in my Travelling Trunk Series. I have a lot of fun writing about interesting places in the world. If you go to my website: https://missytarantino.com you can join my mailing list for bonus stories and be the first to know when I write a new book.

Happy reading!

Missy

Chapter 1

Boredom

Carla sat on the couch with her knees up. Her attention was focused on her new purple tablet. The game she was playing was called "Where in the World is Bingo?" She studied the world map carefully.

"Grandma, where is Brazil?" she asked.

Carla's grandma looked up from the book she was reading. "It's in South America. I went there many times. It is a beautiful place. They have beaches, rainforests, and the Amazon River. The people love soccer there, but they call it football."

"Thanks! I found it," Carla said. "Gosh, I wish we could really visit there. It looks exciting." Carla looked up from her game. "Where else did you go when you worked for the airline?"

"I went all over the world to places like Thailand, Sweden, Australia and Kenya. I brought back many souvenirs.

They are all in that big trunk in my room."

Carla's mother walked into the room. "Carla, your hour of screen time is up."

"Just five more minutes, please?" begged Carla.

"You know the rules," her mother said, shaking her head and holding out her hand.

Carla powered down her tablet and gave it to her mother. "I guess I'll go play in the backyard with Max."

She stood up and reached for Max's old worn tennis ball. Just then, a roll of thunder rumbled from the sky. Carla sighed. "So much for that idea." Rain spattered the window.

Carla wandered around the house, looking for something to do. She tried doing a puzzle. Boring. She tried coloring. Boring. She watched her fish swim around their bowl. Boring. Finally, she went into the kitchen.

Grandma Silvia was baking cookies. Ever since she had moved in with Carla and her mother, there were always fresh cookies.

"What's wrong?" Grandma asked. She put down her wooden spoon and looked at Carla.

"I'm bored," Carla said. "I can't find anything fun to do." She leaned her elbows on the counter and twirled her black hair between her fingers.

"Want to help me with the cookies?"

"Not really."

Grandma Silvia hugged Carla. "I have an idea. Why don't you go into my room and look at my travel souvenirs?"

Carla smiled. "Can I really? Thank you, Grandma!"

"Be careful with them," Grandma warned. "You never know what could happen. The man I bought the trunk from said it had magical powers."

Carla laughed as she skipped down the hall. "Yeah, right, Grandma. You're just telling stories."

Chapter 2

The Traveling Trunk

Carla stopped in front of Grandma's bedroom door. There was a giant poster taped to it. An airplane with a red and green stripe on its side was flying over an island covered with green trees. The words on it said, "Travel the world. Make new friends."

She opened the door. The flowery smell of Grandma's perfume filled her nose. The walls were painted a sunny yellow and were covered with posters that showed places she had been when she worked for the airline. On the dresser was a picture of Carla's whole family on the shore of a nearby lake. The cover on the bed had giant sunflowers on it. Sunflowers were Grandma Silvia's favorite flower. They were Carla's favorite, too. Standing at the foot of the bed was a large black box with a curved lid.

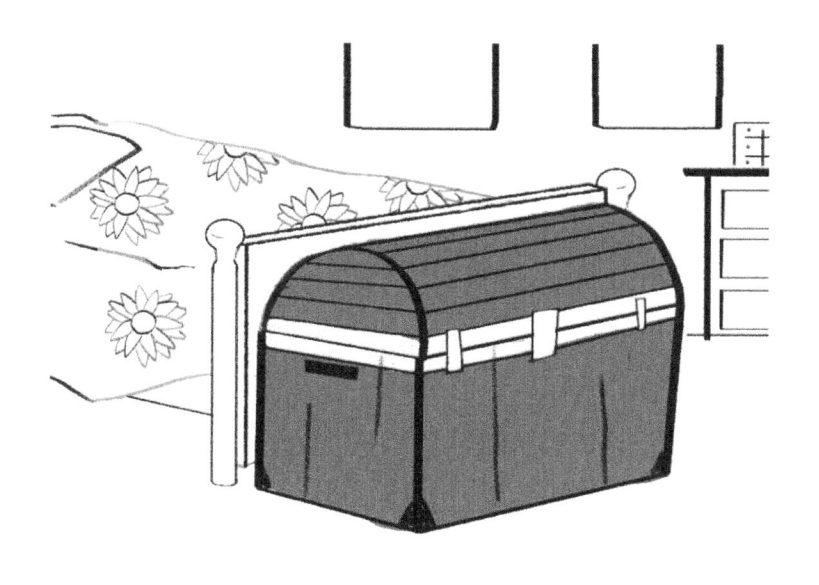

She crossed the room and stood in front of the trunk. She grabbed the silver latch and lifted it slowly. The hinges creaked loudly. A faint smell of roses wafted out. She was excited to see what was inside, but wanted to make the moment last.

At first, all she saw was clothes. Folded neatly on the top was the uniform that Grandma had worn when she worked as a flight attendant. A white shirt, a blue skirt, a green bandana. Carla knelt down on the floor to get a closer look.

Something bright red, yellow, and blue in the corner caught her eye. She moved the clothes to the side and picked up a long piece of fabric. It was covered with shapes like triangles, rectangles and squares. There were long strings like tassels on the ends. She stood up and held one end in her hand over her head. It was longer than she was tall.

"What is this?" Carla asked.

Looking at herself in the mirror, she draped it across her arms. Then she tried hanging it around her shoulders. Finally, she wrapped it around and around her waist.

Turning slowly, she smiled. "I wonder where in the world this came from."

Suddenly a bright flash of light came from the trunk and the bedroom door slammed shut. Carla screamed!

Carla heard a strange sound coming from outside the bedroom door. BOOM, BOOM, BOOM!

She ran to the door and opened it. Instead of seeing the hallway outside the bedroom door, she saw a sidewalk, a street and buildings!

Chapter 3

Antigua

Carla stood in the doorway with her mouth open. She saw a busy street filled with people dancing to loud music. Some of them were wearing costumes and masks.

"What just happened?" she gasped.

Carla took a step through the doorway to get a better look. BAM!

Someone ran right into her and knocked her to the ground!

When Carla sat up, she saw a boy who was about her age sitting on the ground, rubbing his arm. All around them were the spilled contents of his grocery bags. A head of lettuce rolled one way, an onion rolled another way. A bunch of beets had landed at Carla's feet. A pink package with something white poked out of one of the bags.

Carla and the boy both stood up. The boy started talking.

"¡Lo siento mucho!" he said.

"What?" said Carla.

"¡Lo siento mucho!" he said again.

Carla shook her head. "I don't understand." Her eyes started filling with tears.

The boy smiled. "You speak English! I said I am so sorry. I did not mean to run into you." He bent down and started picking up the spilled items.

Carla wiped her eyes and bent down to help him. Soon they had everything back in its place.

Carla took a deep breath and handed the boy the last bag. "I'm Carla," she said.

"My name is Matias," the boy said, smiling. "Thank you for helping me."

"You're welcome." Carla paused and looked around at the people dancing on the street. "Can I ask you a question?"

"Yes," said Matias.

"Where are we? Something strange happened and I don't know how I got here." Her voice was small and scared.

"Antigua," said Matias.

"Antigua? I've never heard of it. Is it by Denver?" Carla looked up and down the busy street.

Now it was Matias's turn to be confused. He scratched his head. "Denver? Where is that?"

"You know, Denver. The capital of Colorado," Carla said.

Matias laughed. "Colorado? In the United States? You are not there. You are in Guatemala!"

Carla's eyes got very wide. Her mouth opened and closed, but no sound came out. She sat back down on the sidewalk and leaned her head against the building.

"Are you not well?" Matias asked.

Shaking her head, Carla said, "No! How did this happen? I was just in my grandmother's room looking in her trunk. There was this flash of light and the door slammed shut. I opened the door and ran into you!"

"That is most interesting" said Matias.

"How am I going to get back home?" Carla asked. "I don't even know how I got here! What's going to happen if I can't get back there? What will my mom and grandma think?" She covered her face with her hands.

"Maybe my mother can help you. She always helps me when I have a problem." Matias reached out his hand.

Carla let him help her up. "Do you think she would?" She sniffed away some more tears.

"Yes."

Matias and Carla walked up the busy street and stopped at the corner. Soon a large colorful bus stopped and opened its door. It looked like a school bus except that it had blue and purple and white and green stripes. The two children climbed on and found a seat near the front. Carla stared at all the posters and decorations and strings of light.

Chapter 4

The Worry Doll

"This is so cool!" Carla said over the loud music blaring from the speakers over the driver's head.

"We call this the Chicken Bus," Matias said. The bus bounced hard as it rounded a corner.

"Why do you call it that?"

Matias shrugged. "I do not know. Maybe because sometimes people bring their chickens with them on the bus. They bring other animals, as well."

Carla laughed. For the rest of the trip, Matias pointed out colorful murals painted on the sides of buildings, grassy parks and interesting statues scattered throughout the city. He also pointed out the giant volcano off in the distance.

"That is Vulcan de Fuego," Matias explained. "We have three volcanoes around us, but that one is my favorite."

"Why?" Carla asked.

"Because there is always smoke coming out of the top."

Soon the bus stopped and Matias motioned for Carla to get off with him. They walked on the rounded stones of the street a few blocks. They passed rows of houses that were all hooked together.

Houses that were painted bright colors. There were red, yellow, blue, and even orange and green ones. They all looked the same. The only thing different was the kind of flowers in the flower boxes under the windows.

Soon Matias stopped in front of a carved wooden door in a yellow wall. He turned the handle and motioned for Carla to step inside.

Carla blinked her eyes. She couldn't believe what she was seeing. Walking through that door had been like walking into a whole different world. The street outside made everything look plain. On the inside of the wall, Carla turned slowly to take in the beautiful patio, the covered walkways, the arched doors. The deep red tiles were shiny and clean. There was a grassy area in the middle with a stone fountain that created a calming sound.

Carla followed Matias through one of the arched doorways. Stepping into the cool, dark space, Carla took a deep breath. They were in the kitchen and something smelled delicious! There were several women there, each one working at a counter on some type of dish. Matias put the bags of groceries on the table and hugged one of the women. She had long black hair tied up in a bun. She was wearing a colorful top covered with triangles and squares. Her skirt was long and around her waist was a belt that looked a lot like the one that Carla was wearing!

In Spanish, Matias said, "Mother this is Carla. She is lost and needs our help."

Matias's mother turned to Carla and hugged her. She spoke quickly to Matias.

"My mother says welcome to our home. Her name is Valeria," Matias said.

Carla explained her problem with help from Matias, "Well, I was trying on some clothes from my grandmother's trunk. I put on this belt and was wondering where it came from. The door slammed shut. I heard a noise and when I opened the door, I was here in Guatemala. I stepped outside and ran into Matias."

Valeria smiled. She and Matias spoke to each other again.

"She would like to help you get back to your family. But first, maybe you would like to join our family in celebrating Día de los Muertos?" asked Matias

"What is that?" Carla asked.

"Every year we remember our loved ones who have died and we celebrate their lives. Now that we have brought the rest of the food, we are just about ready for our feast."

Carla's stomach grumbled. "I would love to join you," she said.

An older woman who was shorter than Carla came up and hugged her. She took Carla's hand and gave her a small doll made of tiny sticks covered with brightly colored yarn.

Carla looked at the doll in her hand. She looked at Matias. He smiled and said, "That is my Grandma Martina. She just gave you a worry doll. You talk to the doll about what is worrying you. Then you put it in your pocket, and it will worry for you!"

Carla tucked the doll into the pocket of her shorts and patted it. "I hope this works," she muttered to herself.

Chapter 5

Fiesta!

Valeria, Grandmother Marina, along with the other women, who were Matias's aunts, gathered up baskets full of food, drinks and other items and headed out the door. They were joined by other members of Matias's family including his father, his uncles, and his cousins.

They walked up the street, laughing and singing and talking with the many other families that were going in the same direction. Carla walked silently, listening to the conversations around her, trying to understand what they were saying.

Carla said, "Where is everyone going? Is there a party?"

"Yes," Matias said. "We are all going to have a fiesta at the cemetery."

"At the cemetery?" Carla asked. "Why would you want to have a party at the cemetery?"

"We go every year to remember the people we loved that have died. Their souls come and join us," Matias said. "This is my favorite holiday. Our whole family is together."

Soon they arrived at the cemetery and gathered around the crosses and headstones that marked the graves.

Cans of paint appeared, and in a little while, the grave stones were bright and colorful. Bright yellow and orange marigold flowers were placed on the graves, making them look like they were covered with cheerful blankets. The whole place looked bright and happy. The people chatted with each other, laughing and sharing stories. Carla loved watching how they smiled at each other.

Everyone found a spot to sit and plates were handed around. A large cloth was spread and candles were lit. Everyone took a cup of water and poured a little on the ground before drinking. Then a giant platter of salad was placed on the cloth. The salad was made of more things than Carla could count. She could see slices of meat, cheese, pickled baby corn, sausage, and beets to name a few. All the ingredients were arranged to make the salad look like a giant flower.

Matias's mother invited Carla to have some. Matias said, "It is called fiambre. We only make it one time every year. It is a tradition to eat it with the souls of our loved ones during Día De Los Muertos."

Everything was delicious. Carla ate a little of everything, even if she didn't recognize it. At the end of the meal, Matias's mother opened the pink package Carla had seen and gave each of them a candy called a sugar skull. It was shaped just like a real skull but was decorated with designs in bright pinks, oranges, greens and blue. Carla took hers and licked it. It was pure sugar, just like a sugar cube.

Matias's mother spoke in Spanish to Carla. She turned to Matias for help understanding her. He said, "During Día De Los Muertos we use the fire, water, earth and air. We light candles to guide our loved ones back to us. We pour the water on the ground. We eat food from the earth and decorate with the flowers. Soon, you will see how we use the air."

Carla couldn't wait to see what the next part of the celebration was like.

As they cleaned up after the meal, Carla felt something poking her leg. She felt in her pocket and pulled out the worry doll. She smiled. *It must be working*, she thought. *I'm not worried at all!*

Chapter 6

Kite Festival

When everything was cleaned up around the graves, the family headed out of the cemetery. They walked down a hill to a huge field on the edge of town. There were people everywhere! Carla could see giant shapes among the crowd, but couldn't tell what they were.

She pointed. "Matias, what are those?"

"Those are kites!" Matias said excitedly. "This is a favorite part of the day. Every year people build these very big kites and try to fly them."

Some of the kites were taller than a house. There were round ones with faces on them. There were bird-shaped kites, square-shaped kites, and even a dragon-shaped one with its mouth open, breathing fire!

They passed a man selling smaller kites, and Matias's father bought one for each of the children. Matias and Carla found an open area and ran around trying to get them up in the air. The wind picked up their kites and made them soar. The sky was filled with kites.

The crowd started getting louder. Carla and Matias brought their kites to the ground and went to see what was going on. The people had formed a ring around a bunch of long pieces of wood on the grass. Under the wood Carla could see a huge piece of cloth decorated to look like a peacock. A group of young men were busy tying strings from the fabric to the wood.

On a signal from one of the men, the group grabbed the top edge of the kite and pushed it up. They kept pushing until the kite was standing tall above the crowd. A long rope from the middle of the kite stretched into the crowd.

Someone shouted and people grabbed the rope and started running. The beautiful peacock kite lifted from the ground and started flying! The crowd cheered. Then the kite wobbled and turned.

Carla yelled, "Oh, no! Look out!"

It crashed into the ground! The once beautiful kite lay on the ground, ruined. Broken sticks and torn cloth were all that was left.

Matias patted Carla's shoulder. "It is fine. The big ones sometimes do not even make it off the ground."

"But all that work! That was a beautiful kite. It must have taken weeks for them to paint it!"

"You are right," Matias said. "It takes a long time for them to make them, but kites falling down is part of the fun."

It was starting to get late. The sun was going down. The broken kites were piled up in the middle of the field. The giant peacock kite was placed on the top. The crowd stood around while one of the officials took a torch and lit the kites on fire.

Matias's family raised their arms and waved. "Adios!" they called as the smoke from the kites rose into the air. The festival was over.

As they walked back to the house, Valeria put her arm around Carla and with Matias's help, said, "Now you know how we send our loved ones' spirits back to heaven."

"That was really neat," Carla said. "Thank you for inviting me to join you today."

Matias said, "Now my mother says let us see if we can get you back to your home, too."

Chapter 7

The Necklace

Back at the family's house, Carla sat at the kitchen table with Matias, Valeria and Grandmother Marina.

"My mother wants you to tell us what happened before you got here," Matias said.

Carla thought. "I was trying on clothes from my grandmother's travelling trunk. I pulled out this belt and put it on," she said, standing up and showing them.

Matias's grandmother touched Carla's belt, then touched her own. She spoke excitedly to Valeria and Matias. She stood up and pointed to her own belt. "That looks almost like Grandmother's! It's called a faja. You can tell what part of Guatemala it came from by the colors and shapes."

Then Matias asked, "What happened next?"

"Well, I was admiring it in the mirror. I remember saying, 'I wonder where in the world this came from.' Then the door slammed shut. When I opened it, instead of seeing the hallway, I saw the street where I ran into you."

"Maybe we can get you back by doing the same thing!" Matias exclaimed.

"What do you mean?" asked Carla.

Matias said, "If you have something from your home that you can use, you can say the same words and it will take you back."

Carla shook her head. "I don't think I have anything special with me from home."

She put her hand in her pocket and felt the worry doll that Matias's grandmother had given her. Suddenly she remembered the necklace that her own grandmother had given her for her birthday.

"Wait a minute," she said. She put her hand to her neck and pulled out a silver chain with half a heart on it. She showed it to Matias. "My grandmother gave this to me for my birthday. She told me that she would wear the other half so we would always be connected."

Matias's mother smiled. Matias said, "Mother says maybe it will take you back home."

Carla gripped the necklace. She said, "I wonder where in the world my grandmother is."

The necklace in her hand started to glow.

Chapter 8

Going Back Home

Matias, Valeria, Grandmother Marina and Carla all stared at the necklace. Then the kitchen door slammed shut. They all jumped.

"That's exactly what happened the first time!" Carla exclaimed.

Matias said, "Let us open the door and see what is on the other side."

Carla walked slowly to the door and turned the knob. She closed her eyes and pulled it open.

Carla opened her eyes slowly. Through the doorway was her grandmother's bedroom. Carla could see the posters on the yellow walls, the sunflower cover on the bed, and the big, black, travelling trunk.

She turned and hugged everyone.

"Adios! Thank you for a wonderful time," she said as she stepped through the doorway and shut the door behind her.

Carla opened the door again. All she could see was the hallway of her own house. Turning back around, Carla walked to the trunk and took off the beautiful Guatemalan faja. She folded it carefully, placed it in the trunk, and shut the lid.

The lid started glowing.

Chapter 9

The Sticker

Right before her eyes, a long rectangular sticker appeared on the top of the trunk. On the sticker were colorful buildings and a volcano with a cloud around the top. It said, "Hello from Guatemala!" Carla ran her hand over it and smiled. She would always remember the fun time she had with

Matias and his family celebrating Día De Los Muertos.

Carla skipped down the hall to the kitchen. She could smell chocolate chip cookies.

Grandma Silvia looked up from putting cookies on a plate. Carla leaned on the counter as she reached for a cookie. She could feel the worry doll in her pocket.

"Did you find something fun to do?" Grandma asked.

Carla pulled the worry doll out of her pocket and held it gently. "Yes, I did," she said.

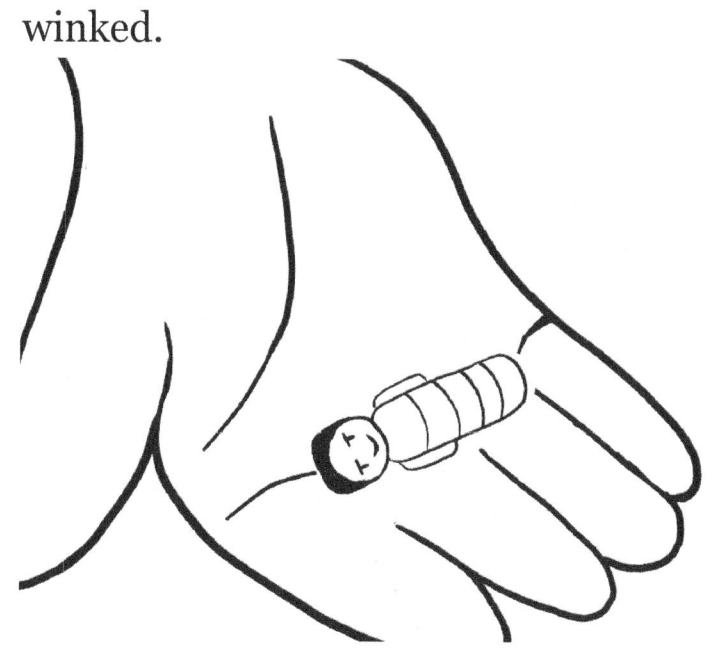

Grandma Silvia smiled and winked.

Thank you for reading my book! Please visit my website to see other books I have written:

https://missytarantino.com/

While you are there, you can sign up for bonus stories! You will also be the first one to know when I publish another book.

Made in the USA
Coppell, TX
10 January 2021